TREASURE SEEKER
BIBLE STUDY WORKBOOK

Discover How to Hear God Speak
to You Through His Word.

RHONDA FLEMING

Treasure Seeker Bible Study Workbook

Copyright © 2015 by Rhonda Fleming

Published by
Hope Writers Publishing
info@TreasureSeekerBlog.com

Visit www.TreasureSeekerBlog.com

Cover Design: Sarah Delaney
Interior Design: Jera Publishing

All rights reserved. No part of this publication may be reproduced, stored in or introduced into a retrieval system, or transmitted, in any form or by any means (electronic, mechanical, photocopying, recording, or otherwise), without the prior permission of the publisher.

ISBN: 978-0-9970115-0-0

THE HOLY BIBLE, NEW INTERNATIONAL VERSION®, NIV® Copyright © 1973, 1978, 1984, 2011 by Biblica, Inc.® Used by permission. All rights reserved worldwide.

Printed and bound in the United States of America.

Table of Contents

Becoming a Treasure Seeker 1

Why I Created This Workbook. 3

You Already Have What You Need 5

The Three-Question Study Method 9

Example 11

Facilitator Guide. 17

Sample Curriculum 21

Worksheets. 23

Meet Rhonda 99

Becoming a Treasure Seeker

WHERE IS YOUR favorite place to spend time? Mine is at the beach. I especially love beaches with sugar-white sand and crystal clear, **extremely calm** water.

The experiences of almost drowning as a teenager (thanks for the rescue, Dad!) and watching *Jaws* on the big screen united to keep my feet planted safely on the shore most of the time.

But there is one thing that will cause me to forget my fear and venture into the water.

Treasure!

Specifically . . . shells! I'm a sucker for pretty shells. In fact, I have a large basket of shells that I have collected over many trips to the beach. They are all very special to me.

There are days you can find pretty shells just by walking down the beach and combing through the debris left behind by the waves.

But to find the bigger, more perfect shells, you have to get wet. You have to go to the other side of the sandbar. To the deeper water where shells have been brought in by the current but haven't been damaged by being pounded onto the shore.

That's where I've found the best shells in my personal collection.

But I'm just scratching the surface.

There are much larger, much more unusual shells available to individuals who apparently haven't experienced a near-drowning incident. Or watched *Jaws*.

These brave people are called shell divers and they dive deep—without the aid of scuba equipment—and bring back huge, gorgeous, unusual shells from the ocean floor.

Now that's what I'm talkin' about!

But it doesn't matter how large or small the shell is or whether you picked it up walking down the beach or dove 20+ feet to find it—it's still a treasure to you because you discovered it and you find value in its beauty.

The Bible study method you're about to learn is a lot like looking for shells. This method will teach you how to discover beautiful treasures in the Word that you will value for a lifetime. And this method will also help you get to the next level as a Treasure Seeker—learning how to find more and even better treasures.

This method can be used whether you're just starting out studying the Bible or if you've been a student for years.

Wherever you are in your journey, learning and using this Bible study method will lead you to a life-changing Treasure: a growing, intimate relationship with God that includes hearing Him speak to you through His Word.

My prayer is that your life will be changed by this Treasure as much as mine has been—and even more!

Keep Seeking Him!
Rhonda Fleming

Why I Created This Workbook

LEARNING TO READ is the most important skill I have ever been formally taught. My Mom taught me that skill at age three. Learning to read and becoming an avid reader at such a young age dramatically impacted my life.

The second most important skill I ever learned also radically affected my life—but in a completely different direction.

That's the skill I want to share with you in this book. It's a simple but powerful Bible study method for all believers.

But first, a little background.

Open Doors

I was raised in church. In fact, I spent more time at church during my teens, twenties, and early thirties than most of my pastors did.

My parents became very involved in church when I was around 10 years old. So that meant I did, too. Then, at age 15, I became pianist of our small church, so I had to be there practically every time the doors were open. I'm not exaggerating.

But I didn't just play the piano for every worship service, prayer meeting, revival service, business meeting, choir practice, wedding and funeral. I was also involved in Bible classes Sunday mornings, Sunday evenings, and Wednesday nights. I also attended the annual Bible studies, where a visiting pastor or professor came and led us in an in-depth study for an entire week.

And when I moved away and was no longer attending my home church, I started going to a variety of Bible study groups and also did several in-depth Bible studies.

So I knew a LOT about the Bible and the stories and the characters. And sometimes I would recognize God's voice speaking to me through His Word and sharing with me an important truth I needed for my life.

However . . . that changed dramatically in 2001.

Breaking Free

That's the year I participated in a Beth Moore Bible study. At the time, I was living in a suburb of Atlanta and was a member of a large church with a vibrant women's ministry. There were over 100 women attending this Bible study one night a week.

The study was *Breaking Free*. That's exactly what I needed to do and that's exactly what I did. I broke free—of a lot of baggage I had carried around for way too long.

But that was only the beginning. Shortly after the study ended, the women went on a retreat and I joined them.

In one of the breakout sessions, one of the leaders taught us a three-question Bible study method.

It wasn't her method. It's not my method. It's only one of many effective ways to study God's Word and it's used by a lot of ministries and individuals. I share this particular method because of the amazing effects it has had on my personal walk with God.

After working through *Breaking Free* and learning to hear God speak to me through this three-question Bible study method, I went from being an extremely shy and fearful person—who was terrified to talk to more than one person at a time—to being a person who was soon facilitating Bible studies, speaking to women's groups, leading retreats, teaching this study method to church groups, and speaking at my employer's annual planning session.

Learning to hear God speak to you is life-changing—and is essential if you're going to become what God has called you to be.

My prayer is that you, too, will benefit from learning this Bible study method. The benefits come not just from studying the Bible, but more importantly from spending time with God, building an intimate relationship with Him, and learning to hear Him speak to you.

Learning this Bible study method and listening daily for what God wants to say to you through His Word will radically change your life.

You Already Have What You Need

Set Aside the Time

I'M A BUSY person. I'm sure you are, too. That's why I love using this method to study the Bible. You'll need some time—preferably every day—but the length of time can be as short as it has to be or as long as you want it to be. That's one of the great things about this method—it can be used whether you have 10 minutes or 10 hours to spend in the Word.

This kind of Bible study is not about doing homework or filling in blanks. It's about developing a daily, intimate relationship with God by consistently spending time with Him—worshiping Him, talking to Him, and listening to the Holy Spirit speak to you through His Word.

If you only have a few minutes, study one verse—or possibly part of one verse. If you have a little longer, you can study a paragraph or a section. The more you do it, the more you'll be able to estimate how long it will take you. But beware of this blessing: one time I studied one-half of one verse three days in a row. The Holy Spirit just kept sharing things with me in that one sentence that was applicable to my life. So be open to all He wants to teach you.

Prayer is the Key

The most important thing you need to do before you begin is to pray and ask the Holy Spirit to guide you in your study and to speak to you about whatever it is you need to know at this particular time.

John 14:26 (NIV) says, "But the Advocate, the Holy Spirit, whom the Father will send in my name, will teach you all things and will remind you of everything I have said to you."

One of the Holy Spirit's jobs is to be your Counselor. That means He teaches you, advises you, prepares you for what's coming, and shares His perfect wisdom with you. And He loves His job! So you can get excited about what He's going to teach you. Allow Him to help you. Invite Him to speak to you and then actively listen for His voice and welcome His guidance.

God speaks to us in a variety of ways. This book is only about one of them. But it is a very important one—through His Word.

Hebrews 4:12 tells us that, "… the Word of God is alive and active. Sharper than any double-edged sword, it penetrates even to dividing soul and spirit, joints and marrow; it judges the thoughts and attitudes of the heart."

That passage says God's Word is alive and active. To me that means I can study a scripture passage one day and the Holy Spirit will point out a particular truth I need for my current situation. Then a few months later, I may study that same passage and He may speak to me about a completely different matter—something that's relevant for me then. That always amazes me.

You Don't Need a Lot of Tools

All you need to do this Bible study method is your Bible and a pen and paper. This workbook includes the worksheets I created to use for my personal Bible study.

One suggestion I have is to take this workbook to your local office supply company and have them cut off the binding and 3-hole punch the book. That way you can keep the instructions and worksheets in a binder, possibly with tabs separating the different topics you study. And you can add more to the binder as you study more of the Bible.

Or you can keep this book intact and write the dates and the passages you study on the cover so you can easily reference it in the future.

Or if you prefer, just use whatever paper and pen you have on hand. The format isn't as important as just doing it.

You Get to Choose a Topic

You get to choose which Scripture passages you're going to study. This can be a person (Abraham, Joseph, Esther, Peter, Paul, etc.) or a story (creation, the exodus, Jesus's birth, etc.) or a book (Genesis, Psalms, John, etc.) or a topic/concept (grace, forgiveness, love, etc.).

Ask God what He wants you to study. He may lead you to a topic you're studying in your small group right now. Or possibly a passage your pastor is currently preaching from. Or it could be one of your favorite Bible characters or a concept you want to understand more clearly.

Since you'll be able to study based on your own schedule, you can take as long as you need to complete your subject matter. For instance, I started in Psalm 1 the morning after I learned this method. I then continued going through the Psalms for OVER FIVE YEARS! Seriously. That's a long time, but there are 150 psalms with a lot of powerful lessons.

Let's Get Started!

Grab your Bible, your pen, and this journal. Find a quiet place. Pray. And let's get started!

The Three-Question Study Method

TO BEGIN, ALWAYS pray and ask the Holy Spirit for understanding of the Scriptures you're about to study (like we just talked about).

Read your chosen Scripture passage a few times. Possibly in a few translations if you have them. For this study method, don't use commentaries or anyone else's notes. You want to hear what God wants to say to you today through this passage—not what He's already said to someone else.

Write down your answers to the three questions (explained next) in the appropriate columns on the worksheet. Also include the referenced verse(s) by each answer. We'll go through an example together in the next section.

- First we're looking for the *Facts* found in the passage. The details. Who? What? When? Where? Why? How? **What does it say?**

- Next we're looking for the *Truths* based on the *Facts*. Principles we can take away from the story that can be used to improve our lives—truths that apply not only in this context but also in other areas of life. Principles or life lessons. **What does it mean?**

- Finally we're looking for the *Application* of these *Truths* for our lives. Taking the *Truths* we found and creating questions that challenge us to apply them to our life. These questions need to be open-ended—not yes/no questions. **How does God want me to apply this to my life?**

- Then every few weeks or after you've completed the study of your topic, look back over all the *Truths* and *Application Questions* and see if there is a common theme—something particular God is speaking to you about.

Example

LET'S WALK THROUGH a short passage together and answer those three questions on the first worksheet in this workbook.

For this example we're going to study Matthew 14:22-33. It's the story of Jesus – and Peter – walking on the water. For your convenience, here is that passage from the NIV.

Matthew 14:22-33 New International Version (NIV)

Jesus Walks on the Water

²² Immediately Jesus made the disciples get into the boat and go on ahead of him to the other side, while he dismissed the crowd. ²³ After he had dismissed them, he went up on a mountainside by himself to pray. Later that night, he was there alone, ²⁴ and the boat was already a considerable distance from land, buffeted by the waves because the wind was against it.

²⁵ Shortly before dawn Jesus went out to them, walking on the lake. ²⁶ When the disciples saw him walking on the lake, they were terrified. "It's a ghost," they said, and cried out in fear.

²⁷ But Jesus immediately said to them: "Take courage! It is I. Don't be afraid."

²⁸ "Lord, if it's you," Peter replied, "tell me to come to you on the water."

²⁹ "Come," he said.

Then Peter got down out of the boat, walked on the water and came toward Jesus. [30] But when he saw the wind, he was afraid and, beginning to sink, cried out, "Lord, save me!"

[31] Immediately Jesus reached out his hand and caught him. "You of little faith," he said, "why did you doubt?"

[32] And when they climbed into the boat, the wind died down. [33] Then those who were in the boat worshiped him, saying, "Truly you are the Son of God."

Facts

So first we want to ask: What are the *Facts*?

Write down the FACTS in the left-hand column of the worksheet. Be sure to include the referenced verse(s) where the FACTS are found.

The FACTS you want to capture will answer the questions Who? What? When? Where? Why? and How?

You can be very detailed and specific or you can just hit the highlights, making sure to capture the main points and any keywords included in the passage.

I'm an extremely detailed person so it's almost impossible for me to "just hit the highlights" because every little fact is important and I want to learn as much as the Holy Spirit wants to teach me. But use your own style and judgment in determining what to write down. And remember, this isn't school and you're not going to get a grade. This is a learning experience and the Holy Spirit is your Teacher. And He's very patient.

You can write down the facts from each sentence or verse or paragraph or conversation. Or if it's a short passage or story – like this one – you can go ahead and write down the FACTS (in order) for the entire story. That's what I did for this passage.

One thing you probably want to do is leave some space between each verse (sentence/paragraph/conversation) because you'll be writing the TRUTHS and APPLICATION QUESTIONS across the page parallel with the FACTS. So be sure and allow room in case those are longer than the FACTS.

Example

> ## Facts:
>
> 22. Immediately Jesus sent disciples in boat across lake ahead of Him, while He dismissed crowd.
>
> 23. After crowd left, Jesus went into mountainside to pray, He was alone.
>
> 24. Boat was a long way from shore, being tossed by wind and waves.
>
> 25. Before dawn Jesus walked on lake to disciples.
>
> 26. Disciples saw Him walking on lake, were terrified, said it's a ghost, screamed in fear.
>
> 27. Jesus immediately said Don't be afraid, it's me.
>
> 28. Peter said, Lord if it's you, tell me to come to you on water.
>
> 29. Jesus said Come. Peter got down out of boat, walked on water toward Jesus.
>
> 30. When he saw the wind, he was afraid, began to sink, cried out Lord save me.
>
> 31. Immediately Jesus reached out His hand, caught him, said you of little faith, why did you doubt?
>
> 32. They climbed into boat, wind died.
>
> 33. Those in boat worshiped Him saying truly you are the Son of God.

Some of you will be able to condense the FACTS to a more manageable size, but that's how it looks to me.

Truths

Next we want to ask: What are the *Truths*?

Write down the TRUTHS in the middle column beside the FACTS they are related to. Be sure to include the referenced verse(s) where each TRUTH is found. Sometimes a TRUTH may be derived from more than one verse or paragraph. In fact, there may be TRUTHS that can only be extracted by studying an entire story or passage.

This step is not as simple as reading the passage and writing down the FACTS. However, it is much more powerful. Look for principles or life lessons that apply to the passage you're studying and can also be applied to other situations, not just in biblical times, but today as well.

If you find yourself having trouble finding any TRUTHS, stop and pray and ask the Holy Spirit to reveal one TRUTH from this passage that is applicable to your current life situation. Then read through the passage again and spend some quiet time meditating on what you read.

If you have a day when you don't uncover any TRUTHS, that's okay. Ask the Holy Spirit to bring the passage to your mind throughout the day so you can continue to meditate on it.

Here are some of the TRUTHS I discovered in this passage.

Truths:

23. We all need to spend time alone with our heavenly Father.

24. Just because we're obeying Jesus doesn't mean we won't encounter storms in our life.

26-27. Jesus does not want us fearful in our storm and 'immediately' reassures us that He is with us.

28-29. Jesus invites us to join Him in a life 'out of the boat' and on top of our circumstances.

30-31. Focusing more on the threatening circumstances around us can cause us to doubt the miraculous life we are currently living.

32. Storms don't last forever.

32-33. Storms serve a purpose—they reveal to those watching us go through them who Jesus really is.

Application Questions

Next we want to create some *Application Questions*.

Write down each APPLICATION QUESTION in the far right column beside the TRUTH each question is related to. Be sure to include the referenced verse(s) each APPLICATION QUESTION is related to.

Example

The most powerful part of this step is creating an open-ended question—one that cannot be answered with a yes or no. This may take a little practice, but soon it will be easy to do. If you have trouble at first, don't stress about it. Just focus on the TRUTHS you found and ask God how He wants you to apply them. You'll soon be asking yourself the questions God wants you to and then you can just write them down.

Take each TRUTH you wrote down and create at least one open-ended question that will help you apply it to your life. Be sure to create questions that apply to your current situation—because that is why the Holy Spirit helped you 'see' the particular TRUTHS you wrote down. Chances are other people will also benefit from the questions you create, but the first person you want to benefit from them is you!

Here are some APPLICATION QUESTIONS I created to go along with the TRUTHS I wrote down.

Application Questions:

23. How do I need to rearrange my daily schedule so I can spend more uninterrupted time alone with God?

24. What storm is currently in my life that I encountered following an act of obedience?

26-27. How does Jesus reassure me that He's with me in my current storm?

28-29. What would it mean for me to get 'out of the boat' in my current storm? What does the 'boat' represent in my life? What would it look like for me to live above my current circumstances?

30-31. What threatening circumstances are currently trying to capture my attention? What can I do to keep myself from being distracted by them? What part of my current life is miraculous? What will happen if I start doubting I can continue to live that way?

32. How long has my storm lasted so far? When will it end?

32-33. What purpose can my storm serve? Who is watching? What are they seeing through my response to the storm? How do I need to change my response so they can clearly see who Jesus really is?

One thing I need to remind you of here is that my answers are not the 'right' answers. The only 'right' answers are the FACTS, TRUTHS, and APPLICATION QUESTIONS the Holy Spirit shares WITH YOU FOR YOU.

While you will probably benefit from other people's answers, the most important part of this exercise is asking the Holy Spirit to speak to you through the Word and learning to hear what He says.

Remember, this Bible study method is about building an intimate relationship between you and God. It's not about getting 'right' answers or filling in all the blanks.

Relax and spend time with God and learn to listen to what He wants to show you in His Word. That's what will change your life!

Facilitator Guide

WHILE THIS BIBLE study method is great for individuals, it can also easily be utilized in a small group setting. Here are a few suggestions for using this method and this workbook to teach a group of individuals how to study the Bible and hear God speak to them.

Planning the Study

- Choose the length of time the study will last. I suggest no less than a 6-week study, using the first week to teach the method and do an example together. That will give you at least four weeks for the participants to practice and progress in the method and a final session to share the main lessons they learned. That being said, this study is also a great way to 'fill in the gaps' between (or after) other studies. Even if you only have a one-week gap to fill, spending that week's class time teaching a group of believers how to do this method will be extremely beneficial to them for years to come.

- Choose the topic(s) you will cover and the corresponding scripture references. One way I've taught the method is to do an 8-week study covering 6 Bible characters. (See Sample Curriculum p. 21.) I use the first week to teach the method and do an example together. Then each of the following 6 weeks we study a Bible character. Be sure not to overwhelm the participants with a lot of scriptures. In fact, if it is a very popular Bible character, you may want to focus on just one or two events that are covered in the scriptures instead of trying to study their entire life in one week. And if the scripture passages for a story are spread out with other events in between, one suggestion is to copy and paste the verses you're going to study into one document and include it in the hand-outs you give the participants at the first meeting.

- Create a homework assignment sheet with the specific dates the study group will meet, the assignment for each week and the scripture passages for the participants to use in their personal study time. (See Sample Curriculum p. 21.) You will need to hand out the homework sheet during the introductory class so the participants can start on the first week's topic and complete their study of those scriptures before the next meeting. Be sure to encourage the participants to attend the sessions even on those weeks they don't have time to finish their assignment.

Facilitating the Study

- Facilitate a time of discussion each week and ask participants to share some of the important truths and application questions they 'discovered' in the verses they studied. I suggest you start at the beginning of the assigned scriptures and cover a verse or paragraph at a time. Encourage everyone to share at least once during the class. Based on the number of participants, you may want to break them into smaller groups and have a leader in each group who is experienced in this study method to facilitate the discussion.

- After you've covered the week's material, ask participants to share what they believe their most important take-away was and what their personal application challenge will be for the next week. These can be used as an opportunity for the class members to pray for each other. Be sure to give them an opportunity to share their progress at the next meeting.

- After the discussion time, I usually have a teaching time where I share something I learned about the topic/character during my study time. This doesn't mean I don't share during the class discussion time. Instead, my teaching is usually on a different aspect of the topic or character, or a part of the story we studied but from a different perspective. And sometimes it's based on a story about the character that wasn't covered in our lesson. This teaching time is optional and may not be feasible based on the amount of time you have.

Celebrating the Study

- I recommend you have one more meeting after you have completed all the lessons. The homework assignment for this follow-up class is to ask the participants to look back over all of the lessons, paying close attention to the TRUTHS they found and the APPLICATION QUESTIONS they created. Ask them to be prepared to share what they see as the focal point of their lessons. Is there one issue that God brought out in several different ways as they studied the topics/characters? Ask them to write down the main issue they are going to ask God to help them address in their life based on what they learned through this study. If they're willing, ask them to share this challenge with the class and have the participants to continue to pray for each other.

Sample Curriculum

Date	Session	Scriptures	Bonus Reading
5/1/2015	Introduction		
5/8/2015	1 - Abraham	Genesis 12:1-3; 15:1-6; 16:1-4, 15-16; 17:1-6, 15-16	Genesis 21-22
5/15/2015	2 - Joseph	Genesis 37:1-11	Genesis 37-41
5/22/2015	3 - Esther	Esther 4	Esther 2-7
5/29/2015	4 - Mary & Martha	Luke 10:38-42; John 11:1-14	John 12:1-11
6/5/2015	5 - Peter	Mark 1:14-20; 14:66-72	John 21; Acts 1-2
6/12/2015	6 - Jesus	Matthew 4:1-11; 26:36-46	Matthew 26-28
6/19/2015	Review/Celebration	All	

Worksheets

Scripture Passage: _____   Topic: _____   Date: _____

1. Facts

2. Truths

3. Application Questions

Treasure Keeper Bible Study Worksheet

Scripture Passage: _____ Topic: _____ Date: _____

1. Facts

2. Truths

3. Application Questions

Treasure Keeper Bible Study Worksheet

Scripture Passage: _____ Topic: _____ Date: _____

1. Facts	2. Truths	3. Application Questions

Treasure Keeper Bible Study Worksheet

Scripture Passage: _____ Topic: _____ Date: _____

1. Facts

2. Truths

3. Application Questions

Treasure Keeper Bible Study Worksheet

Scripture Passage: _____ Topic: _____ Date: _____

1. Facts	2. Truths	3. Application Questions

Treasure Keeper Bible Study Worksheet

Scripture Passage: _____ Topic: _____ Date: _____

1. Facts

2. Truths

3. Application Questions

Treasure Keeper Bible Study Worksheet

Scripture Passage: _____ Topic: _____ Date: _____

1. Facts	2. Truths	3. Application Questions

Treasure Keeper Bible Study Worksheet

Scripture Passage: _____ Topic: _____ Date: _____

1. Facts	2. Truths	3. Application Questions

Treasure Keeper Bible Study Worksheet

Scripture Passage: _____ Topic: _____ Date: _____

1. Facts	2. Truths	3. Application Questions

Treasure Keeper Bible Study Worksheet

Scripture Passage: _____ Topic: _____ Date: _____

1. Facts	2. Truths	3. Application Questions

Treasure Keeper Bible Study Worksheet

Scripture Passage: _____ Topic: _____ Date: _____

1. Facts	2. Truths	3. Application Questions

Treasure Keeper Bible Study Worksheet

Scripture Passage: _____ Topic: _____ Date: _____

1. Facts

2. Truths

3. Application Questions

Treasure Keeper Bible Study Worksheet

Scripture Passage: _____ Topic: _____ Date: _____

1. Facts	2. Truths	3. Application Questions

Treasure Keeper Bible Study Worksheet

Scripture Passage: _____ Topic: _____ Date: _____

1. Facts

2. Truths

3. Application Questions

Treasure Keeper Bible Study Worksheet

Scripture Passage: _____ Topic: _____ Date: _____

1. Facts

2. Truths

3. Application Questions

Treasure Keeper Bible Study Worksheet

Scripture Passage: _____ Topic: _____ Date: _____

1. Facts

2. Truths

3. Application Questions

Treasure Keeper Bible Study Worksheet

Scripture Passage: _____ Topic: _____ Date: _____

1. Facts	2. Truths	3. Application Questions

Treasure Keeper Bible Study Worksheet

Scripture Passage: _____ Topic: _____ Date: _____

1. Facts

2. Truths

3. Application Questions

Treasure Keeper Bible Study Worksheet

Scripture Passage: _____ Topic: _____ Date: _____

1. Facts	2. Truths	3. Application Questions

Treasure Keeper Bible Study Worksheet

Scripture Passage: _____ Topic: _____ Date: _____

1. Facts

2. Truths

3. Application Questions

Treasure Keeper Bible Study Worksheet

Scripture Passage: _____ Topic: _____ Date: _____

1. Facts	2. Truths	3. Application Questions

Treasure Keeper Bible Study Worksheet

Scripture Passage: _____ Topic: _____ Date: _____

1. Facts	2. Truths	3. Application Questions

Treasure Keeper Bible Study Worksheet

Scripture Passage: _____ Topic: _____ Date: _____

1. Facts	2. Truths	3. Application Questions

Treasure Keeper Bible Study Worksheet

Scripture Passage: _____ Topic: _____ Date: _____

1. Facts	2. Truths	3. Application Questions

Treasure Keeper Bible Study Worksheet

Scripture Passage: _____ Topic: _____ Date: _____

1. Facts	2. Truths	3. Application Questions

Treasure Keeper Bible Study Worksheet

Scripture Passage: _____ Topic: _____ Date: _____

1. Facts	2. Truths	3. Application Questions

Treasure Keeper Bible Study Worksheet

Scripture Passage: _____ Topic: _____ Date: _____

1. Facts	2. Truths	3. Application Questions

Treasure Keeper Bible Study Worksheet

Scripture Passage: _____ Topic: _____ Date: _____

1. Facts

2. Truths

3. Application Questions

Treasure Keeper Bible Study Worksheet

Scripture Passage: _____ Topic: _____ Date: _____

1. Facts

2. Truths

3. Application Questions

Treasure Keeper Bible Study Worksheet

Scripture Passage: _____ Topic: _____ Date: _____

1. Facts	2. Truths	3. Application Questions

Treasure Keeper Bible Study Worksheet

Scripture Passage: _____ Topic: _____ Date: _____

1. Facts	2. Truths	3. Application Questions

Treasure Keeper Bible Study Worksheet

Scripture Passage: _____ Topic: _____ Date: _____

1. Facts

2. Truths

3. Application Questions

Treasure Keeper Bible Study Worksheet

Scripture Passage: _____ Topic: _____ Date: _____

1. Facts	2. Truths	3. Application Questions

Treasure Keeper Bible Study Worksheet

Scripture Passage: _____ Topic: _____ Date: _____

1. Facts

2. Truths

3. Application Questions

Treasure Keeper Bible Study Worksheet

Scripture Passage: _____ Topic: _____ Date: _____

1. Facts

2. Truths

3. Application Questions

Treasure Keeper Bible Study Worksheet

Scripture Passage: _____ Topic: _____ Date: _____

1. Facts

2. Truths

3. Application Questions

Treasure Keeper Bible Study Worksheet

Scripture Passage: _____ Topic: _____ Date: _____

1. Facts	2. Truths	3. Application Questions

Treasure Keeper Bible Study Worksheet

Scripture Passage: _____ Topic: _____ Date: _____

1. Facts

2. Truths

3. Application Questions

Treasure Keeper Bible Study Worksheet

Scripture Passage: _____ Topic: _____ Date: _____

1. Facts	2. Truths	3. Application Questions

Treasure Keeper Bible Study Worksheet

Scripture Passage: _____ Topic: _____ Date: _____

1. Facts

2. Truths

3. Application Questions

Treasure Keeper Bible Study Worksheet

Scripture Passage: _____ Topic: _____ Date: _____

1. Facts	2. Truths	3. Application Questions

Treasure Keeper Bible Study Worksheet

Scripture Passage: _____ Topic: _____ Date: _____

1. Facts

2. Truths

3. Application Questions

Treasure Keeper Bible Study Worksheet

Scripture Passage: _____ Topic: _____ Date: _____

1. Facts	2. Truths	3. Application Questions

Treasure Keeper Bible Study Worksheet

Scripture Passage: _____ Topic: _____ Date: _____

1. Facts

2. Truths

3. Application Questions

Treasure Keeper Bible Study Worksheet

Scripture Passage: _____ Topic: _____ Date: _____

1. Facts

2. Truths

3. Application Questions

Treasure Keeper Bible Study Worksheet

Scripture Passage: _____ Topic: _____ Date: _____

1. Facts

2. Truths

3. Application Questions

Treasure Keeper Bible Study Worksheet

Scripture Passage: _____ Topic: _____ Date: _____

1. Facts

2. Truths

3. Application Questions

Treasure Keeper Bible Study Worksheet

Scripture Passage: _____ Topic: _____ Date: _____

1. Facts

2. Truths

3. Application Questions

Treasure Keeper Bible Study Worksheet

Scripture Passage: _____ Topic: _____ Date: _____

1. Facts	2. Truths	3. Application Questions

Treasure Keeper Bible Study Worksheet

Scripture Passage: _____ Topic: _____ Date: _____

1. Facts

2. Truths

3. Application Questions

Treasure Keeper Bible Study Worksheet

Scripture Passage: _____   Topic: _____   Date: _____

1. Facts	2. Truths	3. Application Questions

Treasure Keeper Bible Study Worksheet

Scripture Passage: _____ Topic: _____ Date: _____

1. Facts	2. Truths	3. Application Questions

Treasure Keeper Bible Study Worksheet

Scripture Passage: _____ Topic: _____ Date: _____

1. Facts

2. Truths

3. Application Questions

Treasure Keeper Bible Study Worksheet

Scripture Passage: _____ Topic: _____ Date: _____

1. Facts

2. Truths

3. Application Questions

Treasure Keeper Bible Study Worksheet

Scripture Passage: _____ Topic: _____ Date: _____

1. Facts	2. Truths	3. Application Questions

Treasure Keeper Bible Study Worksheet

Scripture Passage: _____ Topic: _____ Date: _____

1. Facts

2. Truths

3. Application Questions

Treasure Keeper Bible Study Worksheet

Scripture Passage: _____ Topic: _____ Date: _____

| 1. Facts | 2. Truths | 3. Application Questions |

Treasure Keeper Bible Study Worksheet

Scripture Passage: _____ Topic: _____ Date: _____

1. Facts

2. Truths

3. Application Questions

Treasure Keeper Bible Study Worksheet

Scripture Passage: _____ Topic: _____ Date: _____

| 1. Facts | 2. Truths | 3. Application Questions |

Treasure Keeper Bible Study Worksheet

Scripture Passage: _____ Topic: _____ Date: _____

1. Facts

2. Truths

3. Application Questions

Treasure Keeper Bible Study Worksheet

Scripture Passage: _____ Topic: _____ Date: _____

1. Facts

2. Truths

3. Application Questions

Treasure Keeper Bible Study Worksheet

Scripture Passage: _____ Topic: _____ Date: _____

1. Facts

2. Truths

3. Application Questions

Treasure Keeper Bible Study Worksheet

Scripture Passage: _____ Topic: _____ Date: _____

1. Facts	2. Truths	3. Application Questions

Treasure Keeper Bible Study Worksheet

Scripture Passage: _____ Topic: _____ Date: _____

1. Facts

2. Truths

3. Application Questions

Treasure Keeper Bible Study Worksheet

Scripture Passage: _____ Topic: _____ Date: _____

1. Facts

2. Truths

3. Application Questions

Treasure Keeper Bible Study Worksheet

Scripture Passage: _____ Topic: _____ Date: _____

1. Facts

2. Truths

3. Application Questions

Treasure Keeper Bible Study Worksheet

Scripture Passage: _____ Topic: _____ Date: _____

1. Facts	2. Truths	3. Application Questions

Treasure Keeper Bible Study Worksheet

Scripture Passage: _____ Topic: _____ Date: _____

1. Facts

2. Truths

3. Application Questions

Treasure Keeper Bible Study Worksheet

Scripture Passage: _____ Topic: _____ Date: _____

1. Facts	2. Truths	3. Application Questions

Treasure Keeper Bible Study Worksheet

Scripture Passage: _____ Topic: _____ Date: _____

1. Facts

2. Truths

3. Application Questions

Treasure Keeper Bible Study Worksheet

Scripture Passage: _____ Topic: _____ Date: _____

1. Facts

2. Truths

3. Application Questions

Treasure Keeper Bible Study Worksheet

Scripture Passage: _____ Topic: _____ Date: _____

1. Facts

2. Truths

3. Application Questions

Treasure Keeper Bible Study Worksheet

Scripture Passage: _____ Topic: _____ Date: _____

1. Facts

2. Truths

3. Application Questions

Treasure Keeper Bible Study Worksheet

Meet Rhonda

Rhonda Fleming is a writer, speaker, book coach and editor. She shares her devotions on TreasureSeekerBlog.com and works with nonfiction authors through her company RJF Writing Services.

Learning the three-question Bible study method radically changed Rhonda's life. That's why she loves sharing the method and her story any time she's given an opportunity.

Rhonda and her dog Cody reside in Kennesaw, Georgia, where they spend a lot of time at the dog park.

You can connect with Rhonda by email at Rhonda@TreasureSeekerBlog.com.

www.ingramcontent.com/pod-product-compliance
Lightning Source LLC
Chambersburg PA
CBHW080413300426
44113CB00015B/2507